A Better Way to Pray, Volume 1

31-Day Practical Devotional

Shanta Atkins

Shanta Atkins

Scripture quotations are from the ESV® Bible (The Holy Bible, English Standard Version®), © 2001 by Crossway, a publishing ministry of Good News Publishers. Used by permission. All rights reserved. The ESV text may not be quoted in any publication made available to the public by a Creative Commons license. The ESV may not be translated in whole or in part into any other language.

Scripture quotations marked (NLT) are taken from the *Holy Bible*, New Living Translation, copyright ©1996, 2004, 2015 by Tyndale House Foundation. Used by permission of Tyndale House Publishers, Carol Stream, Illinois 60188. All rights reserved.

Scripture quotations marked (DRB) are taken from the 1899 DOUAY-RHEIMS BIBLE, public domain.

Scripture quotations marked MSG are taken from *The Message*, copyright © 1993, 2002, 2018 by Eugene H. Peterson. Used by permission of NavPress. All rights reserved. Represented by Tyndale House Publishers.

Scripture taken from the Amplified Bible, Copyright © 2015 by The Lockman Foundation. Used by permission.

Scripture quotations marked (NIV) are taken from the Holy Bible, New International Version®, NIV®. Copyright © 1973, 1978, 1984, 2011 by Biblica, Inc.™ Used by permission of Zondervan. All rights reserved worldwide. www.zondervan.com. The "NIV" and "New International Version" are trademarks registered in the United States Patent and Trademark Office by Biblica, Inc.™

Copyright © 2024 by Shanta Atkins

Book Cover by Xavier Musgrove

Edited by Shanta Atkins, Eddie Sanders & Elizabeth Escobar

All rights reserved.

No portion of this book may be reproduced in any form without written permission from the publisher or author, except as permitted by U.S. copyright law.

ISBN: 979-8-218-36405-2

Contents

Dedication	VII
Introduction	VIII
1. #prayer	1
2. #validation	5
3. #speaklife	9
4. #beyourself	13
5. #friends	16
6. #thecutoff	20
7. #time	25
8. #hiddensin	29
9. #fearofbeinghurt	33
10. #keepmesafe	36
11. #brokentoheal	40
12. #foolishorwisewoman	44
13. #agodlyman	48
14. #healfromheartbreak	52
15. #selfprotection	56

16.	#Godimbusy	59
17.	#condemnation	63
18.	#love	67
19.	#singleness	71
20.	#dreamchaser	75
21.	#thirsttrap	78
22.	#sexualdesire	81
23.	#inmyfeelings	85
24.	#Godknowsmyheart	88
25.	#Christlessspirituality	91
26.	#gifted	95
27.	#selfexaltation	99
28.	#surrender	103
29.	#lust	107
30.	#isitGod	111
31.	#discerningofspirits	115
A Prayer for Marriages		120
The Gift of Salvation		122
About the author		125

Dedication

This devotional is dedicated to my father, Eddie Aaron Atkins Jr., who helped me fall in love with reading God's Word. He was a bible teacher, intercessor, and lover of the Word of God. When we would visit people in the hospitals, he would pray and quote entire chapters of the bible from memory especially Isaiah 55. That made me want to study and memorize scripture so that even if I didn't have a bible, I'd be able to share with others from memory. My last memory was of us praying, singing and reading scriptures together before he went to heaven. Even in moments when he was ill, he would have me read his favorite verses aloud. His favorite scripture was Proverbs 24:10, "If you faint in the day of adversity, your strength is small." This book is dedicated to him. I love you forever, Daddy. Thank you for every lesson.

Your baby girl and prayer warrior.

Introduction

Have you ever felt like you could do something, but you thought your way out of doing it? Welp, that was me! Always overthinking everything, wanting it to be perfect. When I was younger I used to say, "I want to be a professional quote maker when I grow up". When thoughts and sayings would come to my mind I would write them down on sticky notes, pieces of paper, church offering envelopes, and just about anything. I guess you could say I was a bit all over the place but I kept on writing. Occasionally, I would read my writings to others and get their opinions before telling them I wrote it. I was very afraid of things not sounding good enough. Even with those fears God begin to encourage me to share my words I had written everywhere. The quickest way to share these words was through social media. So, I downloaded an app on my phone, uploaded a background photos and started sharing my words on my Instagram page. I created the hashtags #tayswordsofwisdom and #tayswordsofencouragment and added them to each of my posts. I didn't know how people would respond, but they enjoyed the posts. Many people commented often and said they were really encouraged by the words I wrote and started following the hashtag. I was shocked and grateful.

  I realized the impact of these posts and saw how it blessed people so I sat down with one of my good friends, Tiffany Lynette Anderson, who

INTRODUCTION

worked with me on how to speak and write with more gentleness, grace and kindness. She encouraged me and helped to soften my words. She had me rewrite many of my previous social media posts in a softer and more compassionate way. After rewriting and rephrasing many of the posts it begin to look like it could be a book.

So here it is, a collection of my thoughts, prayers, scriptures and all the words written on sticky notes, random pieces of paper, and social media posts. I went through each post and added a topic with scriptures and prayers to go along with it for each day and BOOM it turned into a devotional. I pray that this devotional will increase your desire to pray, study God's word, and reflect. Enjoy.

#prayer

An example of praying the Word is taking a scripture and praying the scripture through. For example, Psalm 91 says, "He that dwells in the secret place of the Most of High shall abide under the shadow of the Almighty. I will say of the Lord; He is my refuge and fortress; My God, in Him I will trust." A sample prayer based on this scripture could sound like this:

> "Father, thank you for causing me to dwell in your secret place and allowing me to abide under your shadow. I find safety when I am dwelling with you. Thank you for being my refuge and fortress. Help me to put my trust in you, in Jesus name Amen."

When you pray His Word, you take the pressure off yourself to pray with the perfect words. Another thing you must consider when praying is the condition of your heart, which also plays a significant role. The condition of your heart will determine your prayer's effectiveness and accuracy. Ask the Lord to purify your heart through His Word daily so your prayers are not hindered. God is concerned with the condition of our hearts in prayer and not just the words we come up with. Prayer is something that we all must do because we were created to commune with the Lord. We commune with the Lord in several ways, and prayer is one of them. Prayer must be intentional and a part of your everyday life. We are commanded to pray without ceasing.

Many different types of prayer are mentioned throughout scripture, such as thanksgiving, intercession, healing, prayer of deliverance, knowledge, and wisdom. The first time the word prayer is mentioned in scripture is in 2 Samuel 7:27 when David finds the courage (showing bravery or strength) to pray. The example of David teaches us that sometimes we may need to ask God for the courage to pray. In Daniel 6, we learn that Daniel prayed to God 3 times a day boldly, even when the laws prohibited it. So whether you are like David, who needed the courage to pray, or like Daniel, who boldly prayed multiple times a day, we must all be intentional in maintaining a life of prayer rooted in the Word of God. If we are devoted to our Heavenly Father we must be devoted to prayer.

Let's pray...

Father, I thank you for the gift of prayer. I appreciate you giving me access to you through your son, Jesus. As I embark upon this journey, teach me more about your Word and give me the words to say. Lead and guide me to the scriptures in your Word so I can pray according to your will. Help me let go of my ideas of what prayer is supposed to look like and look to your Word for insight. Teach me how to be pray boldly. Guide me through your Word so that I can pray effectively. Purify my motives and the intentions of my heart. Reveal anything in me that would be a hindrance to my prayers being answered. Give me a hunger and thirst for you so I may seek you every day without fail. Please help me remember to give thanks to you every day. Thank you for your courage, wisdom, understanding, and desire to pray. Teach me to pray according to your will and not just my wants. Let the words of my mouth and the intentions of my heart be pure and life-giving in Jesus' name; thank God, Amen.

Let's meditate on these scriptures:

2 Samuel 7:27 NIV

"For You, O LORD of hosts, the God of Israel, have made a revelation to Your servant, saying, 'I will build you a house'; therefore, Your servant ***has found the courage to pray this prayer to You***.

Daniel 6:10 ESV

When Daniel knew that the document had been signed, he went to his house, where he had windows in his upper chamber open toward Jerusalem. He got down on his knees three times a day and prayed and gave thanks before his God, as he had done previously.

Colossians 4:2

Devote yourselves to prayer, being watchful and thankful.

Psalm 69:30

I will praise the name of God with a song; I will magnify him with thanksgiving.

As you reflect on today's scriptural references, what do you believe God is saying to you?

#validation

Have you ever felt like you needed validation? If so, where did you seek the validation that you needed? So many people seek to be validated by money, a significant other, a career, a nice body, a ministry position, or even by "proving their haters wrong." Seeking to be validated is completely normal, and every human being has sought validation in one way or another. Some may have looked for validation in one of the above examples without even realizing it. Validation is something that God gave Jesus when He came to earth. In the gospel of Mark, there is a moment when Jesus had just been baptized, and the heavens opened up, and God publicly affirmed and validated Him. Our heavenly Father knew that we would need to be and feel validated, just like Jesus. God gave us His Word in the flesh and His written word. God has so many scriptures that reveal what we mean to Him and why He created us. He is here to give us the validation we need through His Word and through other believers in Christ Jesus. I am reminded of the moment when my earthly Father validated me publicly, and it caused my perspective of myself to shift, and I became more confident in who God called me to be. There were other moments when God used other honorable leaders to affirm and validate God's call on my life, which decreased my desire to seek validation elsewhere. God knows what we need and will always supply and meet the need.

The enemy also knows that we need validation and will attempt to deceive us into believing that our validation comes from everywhere except our heavenly Father, so we must diligently study the scriptures for how God sees us and seek Him to validate us. God knows if you need public validation and affirmation, and He will always give you what you need. Don't be tricked by the enemy's false system of validation that comes from the world because it is designed to draw you away from who God intended for you to be. Our heavenly Father publicly validated Jesus at the perfect time and will validate you. Stay in His Word and commit to walking in His will; the validation you need will come when you least expect it. Remember that you are an expression of God's heart and creation, so be confident and secure in that.

Let's pray...

Father, I pray that my validation will begin and end with you. Help me to rely on you in times when I may feel inadequate or rejected. In moments when I seek validation elsewhere, redirect me to You and my identity in You. Remind me that I am your masterpiece, created in your image with a divine purpose. Thank you for creating me wonderfully. Thank you for giving me the love that I need. Thank you for making me new in Christ Jesus. When I look to the wrong things to validate who I am, may your Holy Spirit bring scripture to my mind about who I am in you. Thank you for loving me like no other and helping me to trust in your way of validating me instead of my own. I ask all these things in

Jesus name, thank God Amen

Let's meditate on these scriptures:

Genesis 1:26-28 DRB

And God said, Let us make man in our image, after our likeness; and let them have dominion over the fish of the sea, and over the fowl of the heavens, and over the cattle, and over the whole earth, and over every creeping thing that creepeth on the earth. And God created Man in his image, in the image of God created he him; male and female created he them. And God blessed them; and God said to them, Be fruitful and multiply, and fill the earth, and subdue it; and have dominion over the fish of the sea, and over the fowl of the heavens, and over every animal that moveth on the earth.

Ephesians 2:10 NLT

For we are God's masterpiece. He has created us anew in Christ Jesus, so we can do the good things he planned for us long ago.

Mark 1:11 ASV

And a voice came out from the heavens, "Thou art my beloved son, in thee I am well pleased."

As you reflect on today's topic, what do you believe God is saying to you?

#speaklife

Have you ever been in a situation where you said something that wounded another? Have you ever been wounded by words spoken? Did those words replay in your mind? This shows you just how powerful words are. Words spoken can propel you or pull you into a dark place. Words have the power to create and produce things because God put that power inside you when He created you. Words released are like seeds, and wherever they are planted, they produce something. We can often tell what is in our hearts based on the words we speak. If your heart is in pain and sorrowful, you may speak words that create painful wounds. A heart with seeds of bitterness may produce a mouth full of complaints. Your heart will determine what people hear when you speak. We can fill our hearts with the Word of God so that He can remove any bitterness, anger, jealousy, or hatred. You can choose to speak life based on the Word of God.

Satan knows that our words have the power to create, which is why he pays attention to everything we say, so he can accuse God's people and use everything against you. The enemy also knows that we are held accountable to God for the words that we speak. The enemy tries to influence us to speak certain things so that word curses can be released on ourselves or others. Remember, words of death spoken aloud can be used as ammunition to destroy you or others, so think before you speak and speak life. When you speak words of life, you create a better life for yourself and those around you. If you find your mouth full of words that inflict pain, check your heart and wounds. Words of life can transform a heart, a life, and even a toxic environment. When you ask God to fill your heart with love, peace, joy, gentleness, patience, and kindness, you will find yourself encouraging people, releasing joy in conversations without realizing it. Some people refer to this as "good energy," but it is the power of the Word of God and the Holy Spirit within us. Use the power of your tongue to speak God's Word and His perspective so you can live an abundant life and bless others.

Let's pray...

Lord, I thank you for the power that you have given me in my words. I thank you for giving me the wisdom to know when to speak, how to speak, and what to speak. I praise you because my words will produce good fruit and not poison. Forgive me for any idle word that I have spoken. I break and destroy any word curses I have spoken over myself or others. Overwhelm my heart with your love, peace, joy, understanding, humility, and gentleness, so I speak life everywhere I go. I want to say what you want me to say. Let my words be seeds planted that produce godliness and not worldliness. Thank you for giving me the words to say and showing me how and when to speak them. I thank you for defending me from the accusations of the enemy. I thank You that the accuser will not be able to use my words against me because You have forgiven me and caused any words ill-spoken to produce nothing in Jesus' name, Amen.

Let's meditate on these scriptures:

Proverbs 18:21 ESV

Death and life are in the power of the tongue, and those who love it will eat its fruits.

Matthew 12:36 NLT

And I tell you this, you must give an account on judgment day for every idle word you speak.

Revelation 12:10 DRB

And I heard a loud voice in heaven, saying: Now is come salvation, and strength, and the kingdom of our God, and the power of his Christ: because the accuser of our brethren is cast forth who accused them before our God day and night.

Psalm 19:14 KJV

Let the words of my mouth, and the meditation of my heart, be acceptable in thy sight, O LORD, my strength, and my redeemer.

As you reflect on today's scriptural references, what do you believe God is saying to you about the words you speak?

#beyourself

In life, we all experience some form of self-doubt and many people resort to relying on others to define who they are. We doubt ourselves for a number of reasons such as low self esteem, bad experiences, abuse, not having encouragement, support or others to believe in you. There is also a lot of pressure from family, friends or colleagues to "measure up" or conform to someone or something else. But even with all those pressures to be someone or something else God loves and accepts you just the way He made you. He knows your personality, genetic makeup, image, strengths and weaknesses and He still chooses to love you. God wants you to be yourself. In moments of self-doubt, find comfort in knowing that your heavenly Father had you in mind before you or anyone else had a say so. Instead of questioning why He made you, thank Him for calling you His beautiful creation. Look to the author of your story to define who you are now and whom you will become. Just be. Be who God made you to be, wherever you are, all the time. Be the best version of yourself every single day, because He only created one you.

Let's pray.......

Father, help me to place my confidence in You, knowing that you hear me as I pray. Fill me with the comfort of your Holy Spirit. Thank you for forming me and consecrating me in my mother's womb. Thank you for creating me the way that you did. Help me to stay true to who created me to be instead of what people expect me to be. Help me to let go of the expectations that others have placed on me. I thank you for making me fearfully and wonderfully. Show me how to accept who you created me to be so I can walk in my own uniqueness. Thank you for hearing my prayer and answering my prayer in Jesus name Amen.

Let's meditate on these scriptures:

Jeremiah 1:4-5 NASB

Now the word of the Lord came to me, saying, Before I formed you in the womb I knew you, And before you were born I consecrated you.

Psalm 139:13-18 NLT

You made all the delicate, inner parts of my body and knit me together in my mother's womb. Thank you for making me so wonderfully complex! Your workmanship is marvelous—how well I know it. You watched me as I was being formed in seclusion, as I was woven together in the dark of the womb. You saw me before I was born. Every day of my life was recorded in your book. Every moment was laid out before a single day had passed. How precious are your thoughts about me, O God. They cannot be numbered! I can't even count them; they outnumber the grains of sand! And when I wake up, you are still with me!

As you reflect on today's scriptural references, what do you believe God is saying to you?

#friends

Good friends can be hard to come by and godly friends, even more difficult. Godly friends will support you because they genuinely love you, while others support you for all the wrong reasons. Some people may enter your life meeting needs and offering you support while having impure motives. The motives and intentions of the heart will always reveal whether a person is truly a godly friend. Make sure that you evaluate your friendships and ask God to reveal the true friends in your life and those who are not real friends. Friends that do not display godly characteristics, lack integrity and are envious or jealous of you should be identified. When God reveals this to you don't be discouraged or defensive about those who may not be true friends, instead spend time being thankful for those whom God has placed in your life to support, encourage and uplift you. Some friends may be brought into your life for seasons while others may present for a lifetime. The Lord wants you to experience the wealth of godly friendships that bring you closer to Him and align you with His will. If you have been struggling to know who your godly and god ordained friends are just ask the Lord and He will help you.

Let's pray.....

Father, I thank you for placing godly people in my life who will show me kindness even when I am troubled. I thank you for helping me to discern why people are in my life and what purpose they serve. Even in moments where I allowed the wrong people in thank you for shielding and covering me. I thank you for helping me not to hold any anger, frustration or hurt from the past friendships. I release any un-forgiveness from previous friendships or relationships. Father, help me to discern the people you bring in my life and those that you want removed from my life. I trust that you know what is best for me and who is best for me. Help me to learn the lessons that I am supposed to learn from each connection. I accept your plan for my life and the people who are a part of that plan. Help me to be the type of friend to others that you have been to me. Help me to love, share the truth, show compassion, confront necessary issues and be Christ like to all the people that you send my way. Help me to love at all times just as your word teaches in Jesus name, thank God Amen.

Let's meditate on these scriptures:

Proverbs 18:24 ASV
He that maketh many friends doeth it to his own destruction; But there is a friend that sticketh closer than a brother.

Job 6:14 GWT
A friend should treat a troubled person kindly, even if he abandons the fear of the Almighty.

Proverbs 17:17 NIV

A friend loves at all times, and a brother is born for a time of adversity.

John 15:13 NIV

Greater love has no one than this: to lay down one's life for one's friends.

Ecclesiastes 4:9-10,12

9 Two people are better off than one, for they can help each other succeed. 10 If one person falls, the other can reach out and help. But someone who falls alone is in real trouble. 12 A person standing alone can be attacked and defeated, but two can stand back-to-back and conquer. Three are even better, for a triple-braided cord is not easily broken.

As you reflect on today's topic, what do you believe God is saying to you?

#thecutoff

Have you ever heard of the term "ghosting"? Many people feel like there is nothing wrong with ghosting because it seems like the only way to set boundaries with people. However, abrupt cutoffs can be rooted in a fear of confrontation or hidden offenses in the heart. I have met and worked with SO MANY people who have the "cut off" mentality when, in actuality, they just needed some space, counseling, and a conversation with the person to deal with underlying issues. I get it. It can seem easier to run from difficult conversations than to confront them, so most opt out of having them all together. But avoiding necessary conversations can cause offenses to build up in the heart and those oughts will start speaking to you telling you what to do. God wants us to communicate maturely, healthily, and without fear or man. It is possible to communicate emotions, thoughts & feelings without anger or frustration.

Once you learn how to confront issues in a mature way you will have fewer situations where you must "cut everyone off" abruptly. You may even be able to listen to understand, instead of listening to give a rebuttal and defend. Even in situations where someone has an ought in their heart because of something you may have said or done a conversation is necessary. The bible teaches us to deal with oughts and offenses prior to bringing a sacrifice to the altar. In doing so we make sure that our hearts are clear of any anger and we help our brother or sister an opportunity to express the matters of their heart. We also position our hearts properly before God because we obeyed His Word. If we get in the habit of cutting off before a conversation we run the risk of being out of order with God. Being honest about offenses, betrayals, misunderstandings, or miscommunications is imperative prior to cutting someone off and prior to presenting a sacrifice to God. God wants our hearts not just our sacrifices on altar. And you always want to make sure God is leading you to separate beforehand. God will use friendships to sanctify you, humble you, correct you, soften you or help you to address emotional immaturities.

Oftentimes people who are constantly "cutting everyone off" or "ghosting" people end up coming back around in the lives of those people months or weeks later. This type of mentality can cause you to repeat cycles year after year. When your decisions to remain or leave a friendship are made by what offends you then you leave no room for the Holy Spirit to give you wisdom in each situation. God wants us to heal, and it may be necessary to get counseling and therapy to address deeper issues within the mind and heart so you can learn HOW to communicate your thoughts, feelings, and emotions healthily. God wants His children to be able to maintain the friendships He blessed us with. In order to do that we must humble ourselves, ask Him for help, deal with the issues and communicate before the cuttoff and reconcile.

Let's pray.......

Father, teach me how to confront the things I am afraid of within myself and others. Deliver me from the fear of man. Help me not to hold anger in my heart towards any person. Help me to address and deal with oughts that I may have in my heart or oughts that others may have towards me. Help me to reconcile to the people you have called me to. Father, help me have the proper perspective of myself and others so that I can have healthy & prosperous relationships. When I feel nervous, anxious, or offended, help me release those things to you so I can adequately communicate maturely. Lord, help me to desire truth and honesty in my heart and inward parts. I want to learn how to speak honestly, truthfully, and lovingly. Lord, let truth and love lead me into the healthiest relationships I have ever experienced. Please help me be emotionally mature in my relationship tips and friendships. Bless my current friendships and help me develop friendships that will hold me accountable and cause me to grow. When there are friendships that you have called me to remain in, help me to discern properly and stay in them no matter what offenses come in Jesus' name, thank God Amen.

Let's meditate on these scriptures:

Psalm 51:6 NKJV

Behold, You desire truth in the inward parts, And in the hidden part You will make me to know wisdom.

Ephesians 4:32

Be kind to one another, tenderhearted, forgiving one another, as God in Christ forgave you.

Proverbs 15: 28

The heart of the righteous ponders how to answer, but the mouth of the wicked pours out evil things.

Matthew 5:21-23

You have heard that our ancestors were told, 'You must not murder. If you commit murder, you are subject to judgment.' But I say, if you are even angry with someone, you are subject to judgement! If you call someone an idiot, you are in danger of being brought before the court. And if you curse someone, you are in danger of the fires of hell. "So if you are presenting a sacrifice at the altar in the Temple and you suddenly remember that someone has something against you, leave your sacrifice there at the altar. Go and be reconciled to that person. Then come and offer your sacrifice to God.

As you reflect on today's topic, what do you believe God is saying to you?

#time

God gave us all the precious gift of time. Time is something that we all want more of, and some wish that it could be redeemed. How are you using your time? Sometimes, we spend our time doing the right or wrong things. Many make good use of time by establishing businesses, raising awareness about important issues, and sharing the beautiful happenings in their lives. With all the amazing opportunities social media has presented, it has also caused many to waste time. Social media has caused many to be distracted by the success or failure of others. If you are scrolling on social media for hours simply entertaining yourself, that can be a misuse of God's gift of time. If your scrolling is full of lusting after what others have and what you don't, that can be a misuse of time. If you are investigating pages of people who you dislike or people who dislike you, that is a misuse of your time. Time spent researching the Word of God can produce an encouraging message that you can share with others. Use your time and influence on social media platforms to redirect others to God, the Giver of Time.

Let's pray.......

Father, thank you for the precious gift of time you have given me. Forgive me for misusing the time given and being unproductive. Help me to utilize my time wisely and do the right thing. Let my time be used for being productive. Help me to fall in love with spending time with you. Saturate me in your wisdom, love, and Word. Teach me to honor you by honoring the time you have given me. Help me spend time with those I love so that I live with no regrets. Expose anyone or anything the enemy has sent to waste my time so I can be more aware. Thank you for your compassion towards me and for teaching me how to best use my time. In Jesus' name, Amen.

Let's meditate on these scriptures:

Ephesians 5:11 MSG
Don't waste your time on useless work, mere busywork, the barren pursuits of darkness. Expose these things for the sham they are.

Colossians 4:5 ESV
Walk in wisdom toward outsiders, making the best use of the time.

Ecclesiastes 3:1-9
1 For everything there is a season, a time for every activity under heaven. ² A time to be born and a time to die. A time to plant and a time to harvest. ³ A time to kill and a time to heal. A time to tear down and a time to build up. ⁴ A time to cry and a time to laugh. A time to grieve and a time to dance. ⁵ A time to scatter stones and a time to gather stones. A time to embrace and a time to turn away. ⁶ A time to search and a time to quit searching. A time to keep and a time to throw away. ⁷ A time to

tear and a time to mend. A time to be quiet and a time to speak. **8** A time to love and a time to hate. A time for war and a time for peace. **9** What do people really get for all their hard work? **10** I have seen the burden God has placed on us all. **11** Yet God has made everything beautiful for its own time.

As you reflect on today's topic, what do you believe God is saying to you?

# *hiddensin*

Iniquity or sin that we choose to hide and keep a secret can keep us from fellowship with the Father. When we hide sin and continue to willfully sin, it opens the door for unclean spirits to operate in our lives. Many people are demonized (under the influence of a demonic spirit) because they hide their sins, and this opens the door for demons to influence you. Iniquity in the heart and any transgressions must be repented for the demonic influences to be exposed. The enemy knows how imperative repentance is to gaining freedom from unclean spirits, so he convinces people that it is better to hide their sins than confess them. This is why we must take inventory of our hearts daily so that we are not fooled by the deceitfulness of our hearts or the devil's tricks. We take inventory by reading the scriptures and asking the Holy Spirit to reveal our hearts.

While praying, you can grab a sheet of paper and write down what the Holy Spirit reveals. For example, you can read a scripture about envy and then ask the Holy Spirit if there is any envy in your heart. The Holy Spirit will reveal it through the Word of God. We can also go on a fast and afflict our souls so that whatever is hidden can be revealed and chains of wickedness broken. Once God shows us what is in our hearts, we must repent and ask for forgiveness. God loves us so much that He will show us the hidden areas of our hearts so that we can receive unending forgiveness. His desire is that our hearts remain pure; we can only do that through proper submission to God our Father and Jesus Christ. When we stay submitted to his commands, voice, and standards, it will help us to keep our hearts tender toward Him. Even when our hearts become hard because of iniquity, we can ask him to remove the stony heart and give us a new one. No matter what has entered your heart, God can soften, purify, and make it new if you allow Him to. Always be honest with God about the contents of your heart; even when you don't know what is in your heart, be open to believing what He shows you about yourself because He is all-knowing.

Let's pray.......

Father, in the name of Jesus, I ask that you reveal every darkness within my life. Expose all iniquity within my heart that is blocking me from hearing you. I don't want to invite the enemy into my life because of ignorance. Fill my heart with your knowledge. Help me to recognize when the enemy is attempting to use or operate through me. Help me remain full of your Word's truth so that my heart does not deceive me. Show the specific things that are in my heart that displease you. Help me not be proud to believe that my heart can lead me in the wrong direction. Help me not to make excuses for what I have allowed to remain in my heart. Help me to forgive so that I may receive the forgiveness you desire for me to have. Tear down every area of deception and error that has entered my heart in Jesus' name. Reveal what is in my heart and remove it through the sword of the Word of God in the mighty name of Jesus; thank God, Amen.

Let's meditate on these scriptures:

Isaiah 59:2 KJV

But your iniquities have made a separation between you and your God, and your sins have hidden His face from you so that He does not hear.

Mark 7:21-23 NASB

For from within, out of the heart of men, proceed the evil thoughts, fornications, thefts, murders, adulteries, deeds of coveting and wickedness, as well as deceit, sensuality, envy, slander, pride and foolishness. All these evil things proceed from within and defile the man.

Jeremiah 17:9 AMP

"The heart is deceitful above all things And it is extremely sick; Who can understand it fully *and* know its secret motives?

As you reflect on today's topic, what do you believe God is saying to you about hidden sin?

#fearofbeinghurt

One of the most common fears people experience is the fear of being hurt. Whether emotional, mental, or physical, hurt is not what people look forward to. However, you cannot experience life without experiencing hurt. God knew this and had already created a plan to heal you from any past, present, or future pain. People can and will hurt you because humans are imperfect, and we live in a fallen world, but if you constantly fear being hurt, your protective walls will remain up. You may even find yourself running from deeper connections with people to protect yourself from what could possibly lead to hurt, even if that isn't true. Fear has a voice and perspective; if you aren't careful, you will take on the perspective of the spirit of fear. Protective walls made out of fear provide no actual protection from anything. Fear only produces more fear and sin, so fear must be replaced with God's perfect love, which offers perfect protection. Place your trust in His ability to heal you rather than people's ability to hurt you. Instead of magnifying the fear, magnify the Lord who delivers you from fear through His unfailing love. I want God's protection because self-protection isn't protection at all.

Let's pray.......

Father, I thank you for your perfect love. Because you love me, I have no reason to fear being hurt by others because you are the great healer. I thank You for Your perfect love, which removes the fear of the unknown that brings torment. I receive Your love and Your forgiveness, and I choose to forgive those who have hurt me. Help me believe that You love and forgive me so I can reject all fear and torment. I thank You for being a shield around my heart and my emotions. I thank you for tearing down walls of self-protection built by fear. I receive the only true protection from trusting, leaning, depending, and believing in you. I want to be led by your love and not by my fears. I trust you, and I receive your perfect love in Jesus' name, Amen.

Let's meditate on these scriptures:

1 John 4:18 KJV
"There is no fear in love; but perfect love casteth out fear: because fear hath torment. He that feareth is not made perfect in love."

Psalms 3:3 NLV
But you, O Lord, are a shield around me; you are my glory, the one who holds my head high.

Proverbs 29:25
The fear of man bringeth a snare: But whoso putteth his trust in the LORD shall be safe.

As you reflect on today's topic, what do you believe God is saying to you?

#keepmesafe

Life, trauma, and negative experiences can make you feel unsafe in the world we live in. When most media outlets are dominated by negative news and cause more people to fear than feel safe, it is essential to remember that God is our Great Protector. God is the creator of the universe. He created all things and knows all things. Although there is so much evil happening in our world, we must remember that God will keep us safe in this world of wickedness. He promises to protect us in His Word, and God is a promise keeper. God promises to give us the tools and resources to guard our hearts, minds, and spirits. He promises us the comfort of the Holy Spirit. God is aware of how we feel emotionally, mentally, and physically, and He cares about us more than anyone else. When we are reminded of our trauma or triggered, we can take our feelings and emotions to the Father. He wants to heal our emotions so that we know no matter what happens in life, we are always safe in His presence. He is an Omnipresent God, so we can never be outside His domain or jurisdiction. Even when the media uses tactics and strategies to instill fear in the hearts and minds of people, God will allow His people to be exposed to the truth. God will pour out more of

His perfect love so that we are not overtaken by fear of what is happening in the world. At times, God may even lead you to stop watching TV, scrolling on apps, or other forms of media so He can fill you up with His Word, His truth, and His love. No matter what happens in the world, be encouraged and know that God will never leave nor forsake us. When life happens, God will show up. When feelings of anxiety arise, He promises to give us comfort and consolation. Rest in the fact that God's love and protection can never fail. When you don't feel safe, read through the scriptures aloud about His protection and declare it in your mind and atmosphere.

Let's pray.......

Father, sometimes I feel afraid, and my emotions get the best of me, but help me to remember that you are always with me. Thank you for being my protector against all evil. Help me to trust in your omnipresence. When I am triggered by words or situations, heal the parts of my heart and soul that are wounded. Heal me from the memories of my past hurts and pain. Heal me and pour out your perfect love on my fearful heart until I fear no more. Help me to magnify everything that you have done when the enemy uses others to magnify the evil that he is doing. Help me dwell on the fact that Your protection is more excellent and secure than anyone else. I thank you for never leaving or forsaking me. When feelings, emotions, and spiritual enemies try to convince me that you are, allow your Holy Spirit to remind me of your Word that says you will never leave nor forsake me in Jesus' name, Amen.

Let's meditate on these scriptures:

Psalms 94:19 NAS

19 When my anxious thoughts multiply within me, Your consolations delight my soul.

John 14:18 KJV

I will not leave you comfortless: I will come to you.

Isaiah 41:10 NLT

Don't be afraid, for I am with you. Don't be discouraged, for I am your God. I will strengthen you and help you.

As you reflect on today's topic, what do you believe God is saying to you?

#brokentoheal

When we are hurting, God wants us to turn to Him, but often, we turn to the wrong things. We can always go to Jesus for healing when we are broken. God is the only healer and comfort that we need however, the enemy may convince us to turn to drugs, sex, partying, or witchcraft methods, seeking some form of comfort or vindication. The enemy knows when we are hurting and he takes advantage of that by offering us alternatives. When we accept satans alternate forms of healing we we only get worse. When deep hurt and pain go unhealed and aren't addressed, it can cause you to become manipulative and controlling. You may find yourself trying to control the outcome of situations in attempting to gain influence over others in a harmful way for your 'benefit'. When you are broken, it is easy to slip into this error to get revenge or vindicate yourself. Some use phrases like, "Lord, don't let them get any rest until they do right by me," even though Jesus said to pray for those who use us. Hurt feelings can quickly turn to bitterness, making you feel justified in using erroneous statements like this. All this occurs when we don't turn to God in the midst of brokenness.

When broken, we must go to the Father through His son Jesus and stay submitted to His healing process lest we fall prey to the enemy. When we experience brokenness we are not alone and God knows how we feel and what we have experienced in life and He truly cares more for us than anyone else. He also knows when brokenness will lead us back to Him and He allows it. Jesus experienced brokenness while He walked the earth. Not only did JESUS experience internal pain and brokenness but His body was literally broken and bruised for us. And after all that Jesus suffered on the earth God the Father raised Him up, healed Him and made Him new. Jesus never resorted to alternative methods of healing for His brokenness and neither should we. We, as believers in Christ, can be confident that God is our healer and that we don't have to participate in doing evil works to vindicate ourselves. We must pray to the Father to heal our wounds and make us whole.

Let's pray.......

Father, I thank you for seeing my brokenness and caring enough about me to keep me near you. I thank you for healing my pain and making me whole. Just like the woman with the issue of blood had faith for her healing, the virtue that flows from the hem of your garment can heal through every part of my body, soul, and spirit and make me whole. I believe, trust, and stand on your Word because you did it for others, and I receive your healing for me. Thank you for being all the comfort that I need. I put my trust in you and know that you will vindicate me. I'm grateful that you're healing my mind. I am humbled that you are healing my heart. I thank you for taking the broken pieces and putting them together. I thank you for your love, which is the glue that will put all of my broken pieces together. Thank you for complete wholeness in you;

in Jesus' name, thank God, Amen.

Let's meditate on these scriptures:

Jeremiah 30:17 NLT

"I will give you back your health and heal your wounds", says the Lord. For you are called an outcast Jerusalem for whom no one cares."

Psalms 34:18-19 AMP

The Lord is near to the heartbroken and he saves those who are crushed in spirit (contrite in heart, truly sorry for their sin). Many hardships and perplexing circumstances confront the righteous, But the LORD rescues him from them all.

Job 5:18

For He inflicts pain, and gives relief; He wounds, and His hands also heal.

Jeremiah 33:6

Behold, I will bring to it health and healing, and I will heal them; and I will reveal to them an abundance of peace and truth.

As you reflect on today's topic, what do you believe God is saying to you?

#foolishorwisewoman

There are many types of women; some are wise, while others are foolish. Often, it's easy for a Christian woman to place yourself in the category of a wise woman automatically. Let's look deeper into what that means. Ask yourself, " Are the qualities and characteristics that I embody in alignment with a virtuous woman or a silly woman?" Silly women make decisions based on the need to please their flesh, are full of sin, are senseless, and are led astray by their desires. A silly woman never knows the truth about God and who He created her to be. What the Bible refers to as a foolish woman aligns with the world. The world subscribes to vanity, sexual promiscuity, and other forms of deviant behavior. Nowadays, women's empowerment focuses on women dominating men, freeing themselves from God-given roles, using their charm to seduce them, or trying to prove why women are equal to men. These beliefs about women's empowerment are spreading rapidly, creating a more significant divide between men and women. Unfortunately, many Christian women are adopting these beliefs and trends that aren't biblically based or antithetical to the Bible altogether, becoming more domineering, hard-hearted, prideful, and promiscuous, which are all displeasing to God.

God gives a great example of the characteristics of a virtuous woman. So, what is a virtuous woman? A virtuous woman makes decisions based on the truth of the Word of God. A virtuous woman fears the Lord and is trustworthy, honorable, humble, prepared, wise, kind, hardworking, chaste, and often overlooked. A virtuous woman gives to the needy and poor, while a silly woman is only concerned about her own pockets and dominating others without consideration of those in need. A woman of virtue keeps the heart of her husband safe, and her strength is in God. What the Bible considers a virtuous woman may not be ideal for today's culture, but a virtuous woman is pleasing in the sight of God.

Let's pray.......
Father, thank you for opening my eyes to the truth of your word. If I have any characteristics, please help me to know that I have great value because I belong to you. Help me to remain secure in my God-given identity. Remind me that I am royalty and a child of God. Let my decisions be motivated by your Holy Spirit and your Word rather than temporary feelings. Please help me to make wise decisions and live a godly life. Father, Help me to resort to you before making impulsive decisions that could lead me down a path of destruction. Help me come into the knowledge of your truth. You created me to be a woman of virtue, and I want to be a woman that embodies virtue. I let go of foolish and silly practices and receive Your wisdom, correction, and reproof in Jesus' name. Thank God, Amen.

Let's meditate on these scriptures:

2 Timothy 3:6-7 KJV

For of this sort are they which creep into houses, and lead captive silly women laden with sins, led away with divers lusts, always learning and never able to come to the knowledge of the truth.

Proverbs 31:25-27;30 KJV

25 Strength and honour are her clothing; and she shall rejoice in time to come. She openeth her mouth with wisdom; and in her tongue is the law of kindness. 27She looketh well to the ways of her household, and eateth not the bread of idleness. **30** Favour is deceitful, and beauty is vain: but a woman that feareth the Lord, she shall be praised.

As you reflect on today's topic, what do you believe God is saying to you?

#agodlyman

In today's world, many people are constantly trying to define who a man is, and the definitions are opinions based on negative experiences with men. God is the one who created man, so He defines what a man should be. God is the one who created man, and He defines what a man should be. We err when we define who God created without seeking God for the answer. If you are searching for an accurate definition of a man and an example of one, the best place to start is with the Word of God and men of God. The scriptures reveal many examples of different types of men and define what a godly man is. Man was made in God's image and likeness, and the scriptures reveal common characteristics of a foolish man and a godly man. A foolish man despises his mother, builds his house on sand (poor foundation), is killed by wrath, seeks after youthful lusts, and is not wise. A foolish man wastes precious treasure, whereas a godly man follows after righteousness, faith, patience, love, and godliness. A godly man is a man of courage (courageous in the face of danger). A godly man prays with holy hands, is free from anger and controversy, makes his Father glad, and honors his parents. A godly man seeks the Lord above all else. Let's ensure that our definitions, ideas, and opinions of man are derived from the Word of God.

Let's pray......

Men: Father, I thank you for creating me in your image. Let my perspective, opinions, and definition of who I am come from your Word. Help me to seek your Word for answers to gain an understanding of your plan for me. Show me how to be a man who is courageous, honorable, faithful, patient, and wise. Deliver me from anger that causes me to sin or lose control. Shift my mindset to align with who You created me to be and the characteristics You desire for me to have. In Jesus' name, Amen.

Women: Father, I thank you for changing my mindset about what a man is. I thank you for increasing my understanding of men so that I can view them through your lens and not the lens of my expectations. I let go of the world's idea of men. Thank you for showing me what a godly man is and what a foolish man is so that I may know the difference. Let your Word shape my perspective of men and not my pain. In Jesus' name, Amen.

Let's meditate on these scriptures:

1 Timothy 6:11 ASV

But thou, O man of God, flee these things; and follow after righteousness, godliness, faith, love, patience, meekness.

1 Timothy 2:8 NIV

In every place of worship, I want men to pray with holy hands lifted up to God, free from anger and controversy.

Proverbs 21:20 AMP

There is precious treasure and oil in the house of the wise [who prepare for the future], But a short-sighted *and* foolish man swallows it up *and* wastes it.

As you reflect on today's topic, what do you believe God is saying to you?

#healfromheartbreak

Life experiences can be heartbreaking. The death of a loved one, a failed relationship, loss of a job, broken family relationships, or a failed business can bring heartbreak. The reality of the evils in the world can bring heartbreak. Every human being will experience heartbreak regardless of age or gender. So what do you do when you're heartbroken? Who do you talk to? How do you cope? How do you heal? Is healing possible?? These questions may run through your mind after experiencing a tragedy or devastating life experience. You may even feel like your spirit is crushed, but know that Jesus came to mend your broken heart, heal you, clarify your confusion, and answer some of your questions. Everything we experience WILL work out for our good if we love the Lord and are called to His purpose. When we turn to the Lord during our broken-heartedness, He draws near to us. Brokenness causes us to be more dependent on the Lord because we are emotionally weaker in those moments, and His strength is made perfect in our weakness. God can take your brokenness, build you up, and heal you. So why not depend totally on God until you're whole and healed? God knew we would experience hardships, heartache, and heartbreak; He already had a solution before life could break us. Instead of allowing your brokenness to lead you down a dark path of unnecessary painful experiences, turn to the only one who knows how to handle your fragile heart. God wants to remove the pain and give you peace. Allow Him to take inventory of your heart and renew it in His unfailing, understanding, compassionate love. Allow HIM to turn your brokenness into beauty instead of bondage.

Let's pray.......
Father, I thank you for being the God that heals all wounds. I thank you for being understanding and mindful of the issues of my heart. In moments when I feel that my heart may never heal, remind me that you are Jehovah Rapha, the God who heals. Help me call upon you in those moments, so I don't give in to the memories that lead to my heartbreak. Holy Spirit, bring the Word of God back to my remembrance so I can dwell on His Word instead of my thoughts. When my emotions speak loudly, let your Word bring them into balance. Release your healing anointing upon me. Mend the broken-heartedness. Heal me from the traumatic experiences that keep me hurting and triggered. Saturate my bleeding heart in a pool of your unfailing love. Wrap your arms around me, and let your Holy Spirit comfort me in Jesus' name, Amen.

Let's meditate on these scriptures:
Psalm 143:8 NLT
Let me hear of your unfailing love each morning, for I am trusting you. Show me where to walk, for I give myself to you
Psalm 147:3 GWT

He is the healer of the brokenhearted. He is the one who bandages their wounds.

Luke 4:18 KJV
The Spirit of the Lord is upon me, because he hath anointed me to preach the gospel to the poor; he hath sent me to heal the brokenhearted, to preach deliverance to the captives, and recovering of sight to the blind, to set at liberty them that are bruised.

As you reflect on today's topic, what do you believe God is saying to you?

#selfprotection

Many people in the Body of Christ suffer because their hearts have become hardened. Negative life experiences, disappointments, violation of trust, and pride can harden your heart. It can happen even when an individual doesn't intend to harden their hard. When a person feels that they have been misused and abused by people, they can develop a hard protective shell to try to self-protect. You may hear phrases like, "I have to protect me, or no one will," or "I have my walls up to keep me safe. Here's the thing: God created us with a need for His protection, so when we attempt to protect ourselves, we unknowingly reject His. Phrases like the above can be evidence of a heart that has become callous because of self-protection. When we try to protect ourselves, we miss out on knowing God as our protector. When God protects our hearts, we don't have to carry the burden of defending ourselves; we can rely on Him. A hardened heart can cause your ears to become dull to the voice of God and block understanding and healing. If you use these phrases and God reveals that your heart has become hardened, remember that no matter your heart's condition, God can soften it and make it new again.

Let's pray.......

Father, I thank you for being my protector. Soften my heart and make it tender towards you. Thank you. I don't have to keep a protective shell around my heart because you are my protector. You are Elohim Shomri (God is my protector). You are the Lord, and you are removing all the hurt and disappointments that have caused my heart to become rigid. I thank you for ensuring that no matter the condition of my heart, I can always count on you to make it brand new. I will no longer block myself from the healing you designed for me. Please help me to be open and more vulnerable in your presence, knowing that you are my safe space. In Jesus' name, thank God, Amen.

Let's meditate on these scriptures:

Ezekiel 26:36 NLT
And I will give you a new heart, and I will put a new spirit in you. I will take out your stony, stubborn heart and give you a tender, responsive heart.

Psalm 121:5 MSG
God's your Guardian, right at your side to protect you

Matthew 13:15 NLT
For the hearts of these people are hardened, and their ears cannot hear, and they have closed their eyes— so their eyes cannot see, and their ears cannot hear, and their hearts cannot understand, and they cannot turn to me and let me heal them.

As you reflect on today's topic, what do you believe God is saying to you?

#Godimbusy

Have you ever set a time to pray, and when that time came around, you found yourself busy doing something else? Maybe you've told God that you wanted to be closer to Him, and He tells you to spend time alone in His Word and worship, and you find yourself completing housework instead. If you're human, then I am sure this has happened to you. We communicate by our words and through our actions. When your actions and daily routine don't include time to spend with God praying, studying the Word, or worshipping, you're saying, "God, I'm busy." Life also distracts us from some of the most critical things; busyness can cause us to miss that opportunity. We can get so caught up with what's happening in our lives and those around us that we ignore what God is trying to tell us. We may even get to the point where we are showing God, with our actions, that we are just too busy for Him. "God, I'm busy" can look like attending every concert, event, or party we desire instead of spending time in His presence. We can find ourselves attending church services, conferences, and other Christian events while neglecting to spend one-on-one time with the Lord. We can get so busy working for God that we forget how much we need to lay before His presence and meditate on His Word. A life too busy for God isn't a life at all. Make time in your life for the one who gave you life. Get busy spending time with Him instead of exhausting yourself with everything else. God loves to spend time with us, demonstrating how much we love Him when we prioritize our time with Him. Ask yourself, "Am I too busy to spend quality time with the One who loves me the most"?

Let's pray.......

Father, in Jesus' name, forgive me for being too busy for you. Please teach me how to prioritize my time so that you genuinely come first in my life. Help me manage my schedule wisely so that I can have quality time with you. Thank you for bringing it to my attention when I neglect my time with you. Let my desire to spend time with You outweigh my desire to spend time with anyone else. I always want to be excited about spending time with You, Lord, so when my life gets filled with activities, disrupt my plans. I surrender my schedule and my life to you. Turn my heart towards you and increase my capacity to receive your Word. I thank you for giving me a desire for your knowledge and truth. I want to receive more of you. In Jesus' name, thank God, Amen.

Let's meditate on these scriptures:

2 Thessalonians 3:11 BSB

Yet we hear that some of you are leading undisciplined lives and accomplishing nothing but being busybodies.

Luke 10:38-42 DRA

38 Now it came to pass as they went, that he entered into a certain town: and a certain woman named Martha, received him into her house.

39 And she had a sister called Mary, who sitting also at the Lord's feet, heard his word. 40 But Martha was busy about much serving. Who stood and said: Lord, hast thou no care that my sister hath left me alone to serve? speak to her therefore, that she help me. 41 And the Lord answering, said to her: Martha, Martha, thou art careful, and art troubled about many things: 42 But one thing is necessary. Mary hath chosen the best part, which shall not be taken away from her.

As you reflect on today's topic, what do you believe God is saying to you?

#condemnation

Many people walk around feeling condemned. When people feel condemned, they may not know why. They may believe that someone else's actions are causing these feelings and thoughts of condemnation. Most may not see their actions or choices as a cause of these condemning thoughts and feelings. However, the Bible says that condemnation is chosen darkness, following the ways of the world and ultimately rejecting the light of Christ in some way. It's possible to reject the light of Christ and not even realize it. When your thinking, speaking, and actions align with the world, you have chosen darkness but also rejected Christ. Christ loves His people so much that He died on the cross for all of our sinful choices so that we wouldn't have to be condemned. He knew that many would choose darkness, and He endured the suffering and crucifixion anyway simply because He loves us. When we embrace the love that Christ has for us, it will influence the choices we make, the way we think and the things we come into agreement with. We will begin choosing righteousness and rejecting the dark ways of the world. As believers in Christ, we must pray that our eyes, and the eyes of those who don't believe, are opened by a love encounter with

Jesus. Choosing Christ daily and His righteousness leads to a life free of condemnation. A spirit of condemnation is invited into our lives when we choose darkness. However, the spirit of condemnation is subject to the authority of Jesus Christ, so when you remain in him, you can defeat thoughts, feelings, and even condemning words. Remaining in Christ is the key to living a condemnation-free life.

Let's pray.......

Father, in the name of Jesus, thank you for loving me even when I chose darkness. Thank you for loving me enough to die for my sins on the cross. Thank you for teaching me what righteousness looks like through your Word. Please teach me how to walk like you did, resist sin like you did, and submit to the will of the Father. Lord, help me walk with the Holy Spirit daily instead of fulfilling the flesh. Please help me decide to walk on the path of light that leads to your goodness and mercy. Teach me to overcome the darkness with light so that condemnation will no longer hold me captive. Deliver me from the mindset that makes me believe I must walk in condemnation. Your Word says there is no condemnation for those in Christ Jesus, so help me to remain in YOU! I ask all these things knowing that you will answer in Jesus' name, Amen.

Let's meditate on these scriptures:

John 3:17-18 ESV

17 For God did not send His Son into the world to condemn the world, but to save the world through Him. **18** Whoever believes in Him is not condemned, but whoever does not believe has already been condemned, because he has not believed in the name of God's one and only Son.

Romans 8:1 ESV

There is therefore now no **condemnation** for those who are in Christ Jesus.

Romans 5:18 NKJV

Therefore, as one trespass led to condemnation for all men, so one act of righteousness leads to justification and life for all men

As you reflect on today's topic, what do you believe God is saying to you?

#love

We are all born with a need to love and be loved. In many instances, people seek love in people, relationships, and friendships. When those friendships or relationships fail to meet our need to be loved, it is easy to believe that real love doesn't exist. Consequently, some may not know how to love you or how you need to be loved, but God does. Some people we expected to love us honestly didn't know how to, and while this may seem like an excuse to those who may have mishandled you, it is true in many cases. I have sat with, ministered to, and counseled countless people who truly believed that they did everything they could to love a person the way they needed to be loved, but when I spoke to the other person involved, they disagreed. In these situations, I found that many people have entirely different definitions of love. In many cases, people don't even love themselves or their families. All of these scenarios and situations had a commonality: people sought love from people instead of seeking God to receive His love. People sought healing from others because they were deeply wounded by those closest to them as a child.

The truth is that God is love and the distributor of it. Love doesn't exist without Him. Searching for the love only He can give through someone else will leave you disappointed and dissatisfied every time. His all-consuming love is the only love capable of providing you with the security, healing, and confidence you need. God is love, and all His creation is the recipient of it, but when we don't position ourselves to receive love from Him, we won't believe it. If you find yourself constantly seeking love through friendships and romantic relationships, remember that the love you experience from those will never compare to the love God has and will always have for you. God's love will never fail you.

Let's pray.......
Father God, in the name of Jesus, I thank you for loving me. Help me to remember just how much you love me. Help me to focus more on the love that you have for me. Teach me how to receive your perfect love. Go to every part of my heart and flood it with your love. Please help me to always seek you above all else. I want to be led by your love. I ask for forgiveness for prioritizing love from people above your love. Thank you for your unfailing love that heals all my wounds, disappointments, pain, and brokenness. Saturate me, surround me, and overwhelm me with your love. Pour out your unconditional love on me and in me. Help me to dwell on the fact that you love me more, and even when your love doesn't feel good, help me to know that it is just what I need. Your love corrects, comforts, protects, and chastises, so help me see that this type of love I need. I ask all these things in Jesus' name; thank God, Amen.

Let's meditate on these scriptures:

Romans 8:38 NLT

And I am convinced that nothing can ever separate us from God's love. Neither death nor life, neither angels nor demons, neither our fears for today nor our worries about tomorrow.

1 John 4:7-9

Beloved, let us love one another, for love is from God, and whoever loves has been born of God and knows God. Anyone who does not love does not know God, because God is love. In this the love of God was made manifest among us, that God sent his only Son into the world, so that we might live through him.

1 John 4:16 NLT

We know how much God loves us, and we have put our trust in his love. God is love, and all who live in love live in God, and God lives in them.

As you reflect on today's topic, what do you believe God is saying to you?

#singleness

As a single person, you may wonder if or when you will get married. Being single today can be difficult, especially if married couples surround you constantly. Singleness can sometimes feel like God is not hearing your prayers or giving you the desires of your heart. However, God knows what we desire and what we need. He loves us, and He will bless us in time. Some may enjoy singleness and view it as a gift, while others see it as a curse. Wherever you are within these extremes, know that the love of God can and will sustain you. Singleness is an opportunity to remain devoted to the Father and see how you may please Him. If you are single, trust the Lord in your singleness, be content, serve the Lord with all your heart, study the Word, and remain in Him until the time comes for God to change your marital status if that is His plan for your life.

Let's pray.......

Father, I thank you for establishing your sovereign will in my life. Thank you for teaching me to be content in my singleness. Help me see singleness as a gift and an opportunity to draw closer to and please you.

Thank you for the gift of contentment. I choose to be content in my singleness and fulfill your plans for my life. You manifest all good things. I thank you that when I walk upright before you, there is no good thing that you will withhold from me. I do not have to worry, doubt, or fear marriage because you created it, and it is honorable in your sight. I thank you for blessing me with an honorable and beautiful marriage. The only marriage I desire to be in is the one that you designed for me. Thank you that I have complete clarity and am confident in who you have chosen to be my spouse.

Let's meditate on these scriptures:
Matthew 19:10-12 MSG

But Jesus said, "Not everyone is mature enough to live a married life. It requires a certain aptitude and grace. Marriage isn't for everyone. Some, from birth seemingly, never give marriage a thought. Others never get asked—or accepted. And some decide not to get married for kingdom reasons. But if you're capable of growing into the largeness of marriage, do it."

1 Corinthians 7:8

To the unmarried and the widows I say that it is good for them to remain single, as I am.

1 Corinthians 7:32-33 NLT

32 I want you to be free from the concerns of this life. An unmarried man can spend his time doing the Lord's work and thinking how to please him. **33** But a married man has to think about his earthly responsibilities and how to please his wife.

As you reflect on today's topic, what do you believe God is saying to you?

#dreamchaser

In today's society, many teachings emphasize chasing and following our dreams. We all have things we dream of doing or becoming something that we desire to see in our lives. Seeing things we have dreamed of come true can be beautiful and a faith builder, but we must know the source of our dreams. Dreams can come from all sorts of sources: our passions, desires, emotions, God, food, the powers of darkness, etc. The dream's source is just as important, if not more important, than the dream itself. A dream given by God can give you great insight into what He has in store for you, while a dream from the enemy can indicate a trap he is setting for you. God's dreams will align with His desires for you, whereas a dream from the enemy can be rooted in something you desire that God may not want for you. God-given dreams may not be what we may have asked for, but they will reveal what we need and God's desires. Dreams are a gateway into the spirit realm, so we must allow the Holy Spirit to interpret and understand us so we know what He is saying. People, objects, or situations we see in our dreams may be symbolic or literal, so interpreting dreams is imperative. Once you have the interpretation and understanding of a dream and verified the source, pursue it by all means. Follow after what God has shown you, whether it is instructions, business ideas, relationships, marriage, or something that you have been praying for. God speaks and reveals matters of the heart through our dreams as well. If you're going to be a dream chaser, chase God so he can give you the dreams to pursue.

Let's pray.......

Father, I thank you for being my trustworthy source. Thank you for governing my dreams, hopes, desires, and passions. I ask for the wisdom to discern the source of my dreams. Help me know when dreams are from you and when they are due to activity in my life. You know how to fulfill my desires or transform them when they go against your will. Thank you, Holy Spirit, for interpreting my dreams and helping me to know what they mean. Help me fear, revere, and pursue you more than anything else in this life, in Jesus' name, Amen.

Let's meditate on these scriptures:

Ecclesiastes 5:7 NKJV
For in the multitude of dreams and many words, there is also vanity. But fear God.

Ecclesiastes 5:3 NKJV
For a dream comes through much activity.

Jeremiah 23:32 KJV
Behold, I am against them that prophesy false dreams, saith the LORD, and do tell them, and cause my people to err by their lies, and

by their lightness; yet I sent them not, nor commanded them: therefore they shall not profit this people at all, saith the LORD.

As you reflect on today's topic, what do you believe God is saying to you?

#thirsttrap

Have you ever been on social media scrolling, seeing a photo and video, and immediately thinking "thirst trap pic"? Have you ever been out with friends watching people's interactions, and someone says, "They're so thirsty" because of their behavior? Sometimes, people can be thirsty for attention and do anything to get it. We may see someone acting "thirsty," or we may be online posting and sharing "thirst trap" pics or videos. Often, that's rooted in rejection and some form of hurt. What we see as a thirst trap online or even in person could be a cry for help or someone in need of love, and they're simply going about it the wrong way. If you are the person who recognizes someone who is "thirsty," take a moment to think about why the person may be posting, sharing, or interacting in that way. Then, say a prayer for them. If you happen to be that person folks call "thirsty," don't feel judged or condemned.

Know that God loves you deeply; whatever you're seeking, He can exceed your expectations. You may feel rejected or neglected, and that is what causes you to do just about anything for attention. Be careful what you thirst after and who you look down upon. Thirst after Christ; He will provide you with the water that satisfies you. Ask yourself, "What am I thirsty for?" Do I need attention because I feel lonely, rejected, or unloved? Whatever the reason, know that God is always the answer. God will even send you friends who love you and spend time with you when needed. He can also teach you how to handle feeling lonely or rejected maturely so that these feelings do not overcome you.

Let's pray.......
Father, I pray that you would begin to thirst after you like never before. Let the life-giving water from the living wells of heaven be poured into me, filling me until my soul is satisfied. Heal every wound in my heart and soul. Reveal the root of the need for attention. When I feel neglected, rejected, or lonely, please guide me to you. Deliver me from attention-seeking behavior and make me emotionally mature. Help me hunger and thirst after righteousness so I can be full of you in Jesus' name; thank God, Amen.

Let's meditate on these scriptures:

John 4:14 NASB
But whoever drinks of the water that I will give him shall never thirst. But the water that I shall give him will become in him a well of water springing up to eternal life.

Matthew 5:6 KJV
Blessed *are* they which do hunger and thirst after righteousness: for they shall be filled.

As you reflect on today's topic, what do you believe God is saying to you?

#sexualdesire

God created us with a desire for sex; however, that God-given desire and sexual appetite must come up under the subjection of the Holy Spirit. When you are left to make your own decisions outside of God, you will find yourself engaging in all sorts of sexual practices to satisfy your own body or the bodies of others. In some cases, our sexual desires were awakened before time, which could have happened by our own will or against our will. God knows and loves you enough to heal you from any negative sexual experiences. God wants His people to enjoy sexual experiences within the boundaries He set, which is marriage. God knows we have these desires, and He wants us to bring those desires to Him.

When your sexual desire is not under control, you run the risk of giving unclean spirits access to you. Unclean spirits can gain access to you through sin when you operate outside of God's order. When sexual desire is uncontrolled, you engage in sexual practices and develop ungodly soul ties. When you repeatedly engage in sex of any kind outside of marriage, you are training your body to displease God. When you give in to your sexual desire as you please, you give the gift of your purity away to the enemy. When your heart is not fully surrendered to Christ, your body won't surrender either. If your mind is not renewed in the Word, your body will obey your carnal mind. Your sexual appetite must remain subject to Jesus Christ. The way to overcome this is to surrender your heart and body entirely to Jesus, practice self-control, study the Word of God, and heal from past sexual experiences. You can also ask the Holy Spirit to keep you and teach you how.

Let's pray.......

Father, in the name of Jesus, I come boldly before your throne of grace, seeking your help. Please instruct me by your Word. I surrender my sexual appetite to you, Jesus, because my body belongs to you. You paid a price for my sins, and I want to please you by what I do with my body. Cleanse my heart and my mind from the influence of darkness. I thank you that by the power of the Holy Spirit, I can control my sexual nature. I thank you that I do not have to give myself over to fornication, adultery, masturbation, pornography, or any sexually immoral act. When sexual thoughts dwell in my mind, remind me to cast those thoughts out of my mind. Help me to teach my body to obey the Word of God and not my flesh in Jesus' name. Thank God, Amen.

Let's meditate on these scriptures:

Romans 12:1-2

I appeal to you therefore, brothers, by the mercies of God, to present your bodies as a living sacrifice, holy and acceptable to God, which is your spiritual worship. **2** Do not be conformed to this world, but be transformed by the renewal of your mind, that by testing you may discern what is the will of God, what is good and acceptable and perfect.

Ephesians 5:3

But among you there must not be even a hint of sexual immorality, or of any kind of impurity, or of greed, because these are improper for God's holy people.

1 Corinthians 6:18

Flee from sexual immorality. Every other sin a person commits is outside the body, but the sexually immoral person sins against his own body.

Romans 8:9

But you are not controlled by your sinful nature. You are controlled by the Spirit if you have the Spirit of God living in you. And remember that those who do not have the Spirit of Christ living in them do not belong to him at all.

As you reflect on today's topic, what do you believe God is saying to you?

#inmyfeelings

"In my feelings" has become a famous phrase in recent years to describe an array of emotions that all humans feel daily. "Feeling some type of way" is another one—these trendy phrases are used to express feelings that are not easily articulated. Expressing your emotions is a powerful tool and a great way to release what's inside. Take a moment to reflect on the following: Is there a sure way to express yourself? Can you say what you feel in any setting to just anybody? Once we mature in our feelings and emotions, our communication changes. Think about it...when you respect someone, your approach to them differs. When you approach someone you highly respect, you communicate with them in a certain way. You don't just say whatever you feel whenever you feel it. You take time to process your emotions and find the most effective way to express them. Taking the time to be mindful of how we communicate our feelings helps decrease unnecessary conflicts, offenses, or violent situations. God knows we have feelings because He created us, but we must use wisdom when expressing ourselves. It is imperative to season our words with grace when we are communicating.

Let's pray.......

Father, help me to learn how to express what I feel lovingly and humbly. I thank you for creating feelings and emotions in me. Holy Spirit, teach me how to manage and express myself to others. Remove any pride or hastiness from my heart that would cause me to speak without thinking first. Please help me to know that expressing myself is okay, but I must consider whom I'm talking to and use honor when approaching you and your people. Thank you for my unique personality and creative gift. Teach me how to express all those things and what I am feeling in a way that pleases you.

Let's meditate on these scriptures:

Colossians 4:6 ESV

Let your speech always be gracious, seasoned with salt, so that you may know how you ought to answer each person.

James 1:5-6 NKJV

If any of you lacks wisdom, let him ask of God, who gives to all liberally and without reproach, and it will be given to him. **6** But let him ask in faith, with no doubting, for he who doubts is like a wave of the sea driven and tossed by the wind.

As you reflect on today's topic, what do you believe God is saying to you?

#Godknowsmyheart

As human beings, we often use the phrase "ONLY God knows my heart," while this statement is factual in some cases, God can and will reveal the contents of our hearts to someone else. He can reveal the contents of our hearts to others through dreams, visions, words of knowledge, or discerning spirits. Often, we believe that the contents of our hearts are completely hidden; however, as I stated above, there are plenty of ways, both natural and spiritual, that a person's heart can be revealed. It's time for a heart check because God is most concerned with the condition of the heart. Many people are external Christians, but inwardly, their hearts are wicked. Don't master the "look of a Christian" if your heart is not with Christ! Matthew 23 illustrates how we can look beautiful on the outside but be full of wickedness and self-indulgence internally. The Father wants our hearts and not just a good outward appearance. Instead of saying, "God knows my heart," we can say, "Father, show me the contents of my heart," whatever He shows us, we can accept that it is there and ask Him to forgive us and remove it. Pride can prevent us from seeing the things that sometimes enter our hearts. We must go before the Lord daily to cleanse our hearts and fill our hearts with His

Word and love.

Let's pray.......

Father, reveal the contents of my heart and expose every wicked way in me. Address the internal issues, iniquities, and evilness of my heart. Please help me examine my heart instead of pointing my finger at others. Deliver me from self-righteousness. Please teach me how to live peaceably with one another. Circumcise the foreskin of my heart. Everything is naked and open before you, so help me to come into a closer relationship with you so that you can cleanse the intent and motives in my heart. Thank you for showing me how deceitful my heart can be and for teaching me how to be led by the Spirit of God and the Word of God instead of following my heart. I ask and thank you for all these things in Jesus' name, Amen.

Let's meditate on these scriptures:

Jeremiah 17:9-10 ESV

The heart is deceitful above all things, and desperately sick; who can understand it? "I the LORD search the heart and test the mind, to give every man according to his ways, according to the fruit of his deeds."

Hebrews 4:12 ESV

For the word of God is living and active, sharper than any two-edged sword, piercing to the division of soul and of spirit, of joints and of marrow, and discerning the thoughts and intentions of the heart.

Matthew 23:25 NKJV

"Woe to you, scribes and Pharisees, hypocrites! For you cleanse the outside of the cup and dish, but inside they are full of extortion and self-indulgence

As you reflect on today's topic, what do you believe God is saying to you?

#Christlessspirituality

Many are searching for spiritual knowledge, experiences, and "enlightenment". In the age of information that we are currently in, it's easy to find spiritual wisdom, but often, the information is void of the Truth of who Christ is. Be careful pursuing the supernatural without Christ because that is out of God's order, and gaining insight into the supernatural or spirit without him is dangerous. Many have mistakenly accessed the supernatural outside of Christ to appease their desire for "more of the supernatural ." Wanting spiritual insight and experiences is expected. God will allow those things to happen in His timing and His way. He does this so you can be rooted in Christ Jesus, the Truth first. His Spirit and His Word, and He will lead you into ALL Truth, knowledge, and understanding. Spiritual knowledge and experiences are a part of our walk with the Lord, and just like in the bible, those experiences will come when God knows we are ready for them.

This pursuit that many people are on is what I call *"Christ-less spirituality* ."Christ-less spirituality will have you astral projecting, using divination, talking to the dead (necromancy), utilizing different witchcraft methods, and being led by spirit guides (spirit guides are NOT the

Holy Spirit) to gain information, insight, and knowledge about spiritual and supernatural things. Please be careful, STUDY THE WORD, and wait for the Spirit of God to reveal the information He wants you to know. The spiritual world is real and exciting, so wait for God to lead you through the journey of spirituality. Learn about the spiritual experiences of God's people through His Word, like Ezekiel, the prophet who was taken into other realms where he saw angels, or Paul, who was caught up in the heavens, or Mary, who spoke with an angel. When you chase the supernatural or spiritual outside of Christ, you're accessing spiritual information illegally, and demons could be giving you info. Demons are spirits and supernatural beings, too, and they don't want you to seek Christ. Demons will reveal more information to prevent you from seeking answers from Christ. God loves us, so He warns us about the dangers of seeking spiritual information outside of Him. So, let your quest for spirituality begin with Christ, and the Holy Spirit will reveal everything you need to know.

Let's pray.......

Father, help me to seek you through your son Jesus. Deliver me from desires and cravings for spiritual knowledge outside of the boundaries you set for me. Thank you for the power of the supernatural. Please help me to reject any spiritual insight gained from spirit guides, orishas, necromancy, divination, and any forms of witchcraft. I trust you to show and reveal everything you want me to see and know. Teach me how to wait on you to receive knowledge and supernatural insight instead of seeking it elsewhere in Jesus' name; thank God, Amen.

Let's meditate on these scriptures:

Ezekiel 1:4-5 KJV

And I looked, and, behold, a whirlwind came out of the north, a great cloud, and a fire infolding itself, and a brightness was about it, and out of the midst thereof as the colour of amber, out of the midst of the fire. Also out of the midst thereof came the likeness of four living creatures. And this was their appearance; they had the likeness of a man.

2 Corinthians 12:2 ESV

I know a man in Christ who fourteen years ago was caught up to the third heaven—whether in the body or out of the body I do not know, God knows.

Leviticus 19:31 ESV

Do not turn to mediums or necromancers; do not seek them out, and so make yourselves unclean by them: I am the Lord your God

As you reflect on today's topic, what do you believe God is saying to you about seeking spiritual experiences and the supernatural?

#gifted

Every person is born with a gift given by the Creator. It could be a gift to sing, dance, lead, organize, serve, or even the gift of developing and cultivating others. When God gives us gifts He usually gives us an assignment and people that He wants us to reach. He also gives gifts to create wealth for our families and generations to come. However, many are unwilling to fulfill their God-given assignment with their gifts because it inconveniences them. For example, a person may be gifted to fundraise but instead of fundraising to build a local church, ministry, or organization, they'll use their gift to fundraise for businesses that promote harmful products, greed and lust. Another may be blessed with the gift to market products really well and they will use that gift to market products that will seduce people into sinful actions. There are people with the gift to lead and organize, who will train and lead entire operations to exploit communities and nations of people for their own benefit.

All these scenarios happen when gifts or talents are cultivated by the wrong people, wrong environment for selfish reasons. Satan knows that he cannot destroy the gift or talent God gave you so he will try to convince you to misuse it. He influences people to use God given gifts to tear down the kingdom of God instead of glorifying God with them. Can you imagine if the gifts to organize, lead, and influence others was used to bring people to Jesus, to unify families, churches and nations? This is what happens when gifts are sanctified because they are surrendered to God's purposes. Sanctified gifts bring God glory and causes His people to prosper. Gifts can create solutions or create more problems. We must learn how God wants us to use our gifts and the result will always be beneficial to the individual and others. So pray and ask God to reveal His purpose and plan for your gifts, surrender our gifts to Him to bring God glory, save souls, and solve problems within the world.

Let's pray.......

Father, forgive me for using your gifts to please myself and to do evil. Thank you for the ability, creativity, and willingness to orchestrate events that will build your kingdom. Thank you for giving me gifts, talents, and a skill set that will impact the world and lead them closer to you, Jesus. Show me how to serve and glorify You with my gifts, talents, and skills. Thank you for giving me everything I need that pertains to life and godliness in Jesus' name, Amen.

Let's meditate on these scriptures:
1 Chronicles 22:15
There are also workmen with you in abundance, cutters and workers of stone and timber, and all kinds of men who are skillful in every kind

of work

James 1:17 NIV

Every good and perfect gift is from above, coming down from the Father of the heavenly lights, who does not change like shifting shadows.

1 Peter 4:10 NIV

Each of you should use whatever gift you have received to serve others, as faithful stewards of God's grace in its various forms.

As you reflect on today's topic, what do you believe God is saying to you?

#selfexaltation

There was a beautiful angel who had the most amazing wings, precious stones, highly anointed and responsible for guarding the presence of God. He took the gift and merchandised it for his purposes. He convinced himself that he deserved a higher position than his peers and leader. His name is Lucifer, who became so prideful and arrogant that he began to exalt himself above God. and he will try to convince you that you're so beautiful and powerful that you should exalt yourself. He can make you believe more in yourself than you believe in God. Now believing in yourself may seem like a good thing and it can be as long as you believe in God more. When you focus more on believing in yourself, your ability, your position or your beauty you run the risk of becoming your own god just like Lucifer. See, Lucifer is not secure in the position that God gave him and got puffed up in who he was. Self exaltation can look like self-love however, when we go outside of God's order for exaltation and believe in ourselves MORE than we believe in God, we run the risk of becoming just like Lucifer. Lucifer was discontent with the position that God gave him, with who God created him to be, and that led him to take matters into his own hands. He believed that He needed more, more power, a higher position and ultimately God's position. Pride can make us believe that we need to exalt ourselves because we are gifted, talented, or skilled in an area where we should humble ourselves before the God who gave it to us. God is the creator of all and is exalted above everything. Instead of trying to exalt yourself, humble yourself and allow HIM to exalt you when the time is right.

Let's pray.......

Father, keep my heart from being filled with pride. Forgive me for allowing any of my gifts to blind me and get lifted in pride. Thank you for keeping me from falling into the sin that got an angel tossed from heaven. No matter how many gifts I possess, help me always exalt you above my gifts. Thank you for humbling me and revealing any area of my heart where seeds of pride have been planted. May every seed sown by the enemy be plucked up and burned by God's holy fire. Show me how to be meek so I may inherit blessings and experience prosperity that only you can bring. Help me to depend on you more than anyone or anything; in Jesus' name, Amen.

Let's meditate on these scriptures:

Isaiah 14:13 NAS

But you said in your heart, "I will ascend to heaven; I will raise my throne above the stars of God, and I will sit on the mount of assembly In the recesses of the north."

Luke 18:9-14

Also He spoke this parable to some who trusted in themselves that they were righteous, and despised others: "Two men went up to the temple to pray, one a Pharisee and the other a tax collector. The Pharisee stood and prayed thus with himself, 'God, I thank You that I am not like other men—extortioners, unjust, adulterers, or even as this tax collector. I fast twice a week; I give tithes of all that I possess.' And the tax collector, standing afar off, would not so much as raise *his* eyes to heaven, but beat his breast, saying, 'God, be merciful to me a sinner!' I tell you, this man went down to his house justified *rather* than the other; for everyone who exalts himself will be humbled, and he who humbles himself will be exalted."

Philippians 2:5-11 NKJV
"Let this mind be in you which was also in Christ Jesus, who, being in the form of God, did not consider it robbery to be equal with God, but made Himself of no reputation, taking the form of a bondservant, and coming in the likeness of men. And being found in appearance as a man, He humbled Himself and became obedient to the point of death, even the death of the cross. Therefore God also has highly exalted Him and given Him the name which is above every name, that at the name of Jesus every knee should bow, of those in heaven, and of those on earth, and of those under the earth, and that every tongue should confess that Jesus Christ is Lord, to the glory of God the Father."

1 Peter 5:6-7
⁶ And God will exalt you in due time, if you humble yourselves under his mighty hand ⁷ by casting all your cares on him because he cares for you.

As you reflect on today's topic, what do you believe God is saying to you?

#surrender

In this day and age, many people need to be more truthful about what we must give up to live like Christ. Jesus said if we want to follow Him, we must take up our cross and follow him (Matthew 16:24). Jesus told the rich young ruler that in addition to keeping the commands, he would need to give up all he owned (Mark 10:17-23). There will come a time in your walk with Christ when you must give up things you want to keep. You will have to surrender everything to Him. We must learn to deny ourselves and our personal agendas so Christ may be exalted. In order for us to be alive in Christ, a part of us must be crucified. We can't just try to add Jesus to the mix. If Jesus is truly Lord, He must be Lord over all areas of our lives, not some. He may tell us to give up our favorite thing because He knows we are in idolatry. God is jealous of us because we belong to Him, and He creates us. When we receive Christ, we must be willing to give up those things that have won our affection to go deeper into Him. Our intimate relationship with Him is more important than anything else. He knows when we are serving him half-heartedly. He is not satisfied with some of you. He wants all of you.

Let's pray.......

Father, in the name of Jesus, help me believe and serve you wholeheartedly. Help me understand the depth of your love and desire to be in fellowship with me. Let my desire for you be greater than for anything else on earth. Please help me to set my affections upon you. Please help me to give up whatever you tell me to give up so I can be wholly committed to you. I surrender to you and receive you as Lord over my entire life.

Let's meditate on these scriptures:

Colossians 3:2 KJV

He doesn't just want some of you. He wants all of you.

Mark 10:17-23 NASB

[17] As He was setting out on a journey, a man ran up to Him and knelt before Him, and asked Him, "Good Teacher, what shall I do so that I may inherit eternal life?" [18] But Jesus said to him, "Why do you call Me good? No one is good except God alone. [19] You know the commandments: 'Do not murder, Do not commit adultery, Do not steal, Do not give false testimony, Do not defraud, Honor your father and mother.'" [20] And he said to Him, "Teacher, I have kept all these things from my youth." [21] Looking at him, Jesus showed love to him and said to him, "One thing you lack: go and sell all you possess and give to the poor, and you will have treasure in heaven; and come, follow Me." [22] But he was deeply dismayed by these words, and he went away grieving; for he was one who owned much property. And Jesus, looking around, *said to His disciples, "How hard it will be for those who are wealthy to enter

the kingdom of God!"

Jeremiah 31:3 NLT
Long ago the LORD said to Israel: I have loved you, my people, with an everlasting love. With unfailing love I have drawn you to myself.

Ezekiel 11:19-21 AMP
"And I will give them one heart [a new heart], and put a new spirit within them. I will take from them the heart of stone, and will give them a heart of flesh [that is responsive to My touch], that they may walk in My statutes and keep My ordinances and do them. Then they shall be My people, and I will be their God. But as for those whose heart longs for and follows after their detestable things and their repulsive things [associated with idolatry], on their own head I will repay [them in full for] their [vile] conduct," says the Lord GOD."

As you reflect on today's topic, what do you believe God is saying to you?

#lust

When you see or hear the word lust, many things may come to mind. Many would say sex or sexual desire comes to mind. When you look up the definition of lust, you will find words to describe it, such as desire, passion, longing, and appetite. If we see lust as an appetite, it is easier to understand that it isn't just a sexual craving. It can be a desire for just about anything. We are all born with natural desires in our bodies, our hearts, and even spiritual desires. But then there is a spirit of lust with an appetite of its own.

The spirit of lust has an appetite for everything that is directly opposed to God's boundaries. The spirit of lust can influence what you desire physically, emotionally, and relationally. The spirit of lust can affect your mindset and produce thoughts, emotions, perspectives, visions, and dreams. The spirit of lust has one goal, and that is to rule over your body and soul. The spirit of lust can influence you more than you realize, which is why it's imperative to submit our desires, passions, longings, and appetites to the Lord. We submit it to the Lord by talking to Him about it, acknowledging what they are, and asking Him to satisfy those longings OR give us the self-control we need. If we desire something, we should ensure it aligns with what God wants for us. For example, you may want to be loved, held, and cared for. Those are typical human desires, but when we go outside of God's order to fulfill them, we can begin fornicating, committing adultery, or chasing after someone who is no good for us. Spirits of lust, whoredoms, and perversion come in to get you to chase the very thing or people God doesn't want for you. These unclean spirits aren't satisfied until you operate out of God's order.

Acknowledging that sexual desire is normal and simply submitting those desires to God's order, we close the door to the spirit of lust. When we use self-control and cast down lustful thoughts when they come to our mind, we stay in alignment with the Holy Spirit and come out of agreement with the spirit of lust. So, suppose you're having a rough time or simply struggling with bringing your sexual desire under control. In that case, I invite you to pray the prayer below, meditate on the scriptures, and come out of agreement with the spirit of lust and into agreement with the Spirit of God concerning your desires.

Let's pray.......

Father, thank you for opening my eyes to how the spirit of lust operates. I thank you for helping me to be open and vulnerable with you so I can be open about specific desires. Let my desires come into alignment with what You desire for me. Influence my heart, mind, and my decisions. Please teach me how to practice self-control and let the fruit of the spirit be produced in me. Lord, help me not to make any provision to fulfill the lust of my flesh. Lead me by your Holy Spirit and the truth of your words. Instruct me how to identify the spirit of lust in my life so I can be freed from it. I come out of agreement with the spirit of lust and its design for my sexual experiences. I will not satisfy the lust of the flesh, but I will walk in the spirit. Father destroys the sexual appetites that I have that are rooted in lust. Deliver me from the influence and plans of the spirit of lust in Jesus' name, Amen.

Let's meditate on this scripture:

1 John 2:16

For all that is in the world—the desires of the flesh and the desires of the eyes and pride of life—is not from the Father but is from the world.

1 Thessalonians 4:3-5

For this is the will of God, your sanctification: that you should abstain from sexual immorality; that each of you should know how to possess his own vessel in sanctification and honor, not in passion of lust, like the Gentiles who do not know God.

2 Timothy 2:22 BLB

Now flee youthful lusts and pursue righteousness, faith, love, *and* peace, along with those calling on the Lord out of pure a heart.

As you reflect on today's topic, what do you believe God is saying to you?

#isitGod

Everything that seems good is not always GOD. Genesis speaks of a tree in the Garden of Eden called the Tree of the Knowledge of Good and Evil. Eating from this tree is what caused Adam and Even to experience spiritual and eventually physical death. The fruit on the tree Eve ate from was "good," yet it led to death. There are many good things, but even these things must be discerned. Sometimes, you may be presented with what seems like a good opportunity and may be convinced that taking it is the right thing to do. However, if the opportunity requires you to go against what God told you, it isn't good in His eyes. God told Adam and Eve that the tree had good and evil knowledge, but they were not to eat it. Adam and Eve had plenty of other God-given options. Still, the enemy made them believe that there was a "blessing" of "being like gods" (Genesis 3:5). Eating the fruit from that tree required Adam and Eve to be disobedient to what God said. It was the serpent that convinced them that something God said not to eat was good for them, and he continues to trick people in the same manner today. We must identify the source behind specific opportunities and what is necessary to get the opportunity. Every opportunity you have that will require you to disobey God is NOT godly.

Lesser gods, also known as idols, can present opportunities as well, but it will always require some level of compromise. Consider the time when satan offered Jesus the kingdoms of this world but required Jesus to bow down and worship him (see Matthew 4:8-10). That is a perfect example of an opportunity that isn't from God. Always remember that everyone who uses the word "god" does not always refer to the One you serve. If it requires you to compromise, it is the enemy using what you desire to have to get what he wants from you. God doesn't require compromise to receive His blessings; He blesses us because He loves us, and when we obey Him, we receive even more. Ask yourself, is this a good opportunity or a Godly opportunity?? Do I have to compromise my walk with God or disobey his commands to gain this opportunity? Ask yourself, is it good, or is this God?

Let's pray.......

Father, help me to know the difference between a good opportunity and an opportunity from God. Father, remove any idols from my heart that may prevent me from discerning the truth. Lord, give me the strength to reject what satan brings and position myself for the more incredible blessing you have for me. Help to remember that your blessings makes rich and adds no sorrow. Release your wisdom upon me so I can choose wisely when presented with different opportunities. In Jesus' name, thank God, Amen.

Let's meditate on these scriptures:

1 Corinthians 8:5-6 DBT

For and if indeed there are [those] called gods, whether in heaven or on earth, (as there are gods many, and lords many,) yet to us [there is] one God, the Father, of whom all things, and *we* for him; and one Lord, Jesus Christ, by whom [are] all things, and *we* by him.

Matthew 4:8-10 NKJV

Again, the devil took Him up on an exceedingly high mountain, and showed Him all the kingdoms of the world and their glory. And he said to Him, "All these things I will give You if You will fall down and worship me." Then Jesus said to him, "Away with you, Satan! For it is written, "You shall worship the Lord your God, and Him only you shall serve.

As you reflect on today's topic, what do you believe God is saying to you?

#discerningofspirits

Nowadays, we receive a wealth of information from various sources daily. The source of information could be from God, the hearts and minds of men, or the kingdom of darkness. We must be able to discern the source. Every believer has a certain level of discernment that comes from the Holy Spirit, but the ***gift of discerning spirits*** is knowing the source, the spirit, or the motive behind it. Studying the Word will help you discern more accurately. The gift of discerning spirits can help you to discern spirits in a person, a song, a church, a family, a region, etc. For example, you could walk into a building and see people and hear the "spirit of jealousy," or you may sense a strong feeling of jealousy. The Holy Spirit may be letting you know what spirit is in operation. It's not just a feeling; it is a knowing deep within your spirit of where the Holy Spirit dwells. This gift will allow you to accurately discern and not speculate or try to figure things out within yourself. God gave some this gift as a benefit because it will enable you to determine hidden agendas, impure motives, unclean spirits, godly spirits, and those with pure intentions. It is helpful in romantic relationships, business deals, friendships, and churches. Everyone should ask the Holy Spirit for this gift and remember it isn't just discernment; it is ***discerning of spirits.***

Read and study the stories in the scriptures, and when situations arise, God will bring the scriptures to your remembrance so that you can discern the source, motive, and spirits influencing a person or a region. I remember when I walked into a church, prayer was happening, two ladies were praying, and an older man was to their right. I didn't think much of it, but I heard these words: "Jannes and Jambres." I recalled those names from a scripture I studied in the bible (2 Timothy 3:8), discussing how Jannes and Jambres withstood Moses. Jannes and Jambres were servants of Pharaoh, and they mimicked miracles that Moses did, but their power source was not from God. I knew then that these two people were operating in that same false power. However, I wasn't entirely sure, so I went to the Word of God, studied that story even more, researched, and prayed about it. Well, sure enough, I had heard accurately, and after a short time, these two people began opposing the older man (Moses) in the same way that Jannes and Jambres withstood Moses by working false miracles.

True deliverance was blocked for many people because the spirit behind these "miracles" they performed was not a work of the Holy Spirit. These "miracles" were used to manipulate and control people and block them from being freed. "Jannes and Jambres" drew attention to their false power so that people would look to them instead of God. Had it not been for the gift of the Holy Spirit, I would have never known, and I could've fallen prey to the false spirit behind these "miracles ." So, the Holy Spirit allowed me to discern *an impure motive, a hidden agenda*, and *a mocking and mimicking spirit.* This unique gift of the Holy Spirit was at work and kept me from a potentially dangerous situation, which is why I pray God gives everyone the gift.

Let's pray.......

Father, I thank you for the gift of the discerning of spirits and ask that you increase my portion. Don't let me be so blinded by natural abilities, gifts, and talents that the enemy seduces me. Please help me to know the difference between a good feeling and your spirit that comes to transform us. I thank you for your Word, which is a discerner, so help me study your Word more so I can accurately discern spirits and motives. Thank you for revealing the spirit behind the actions and the source of information being presented so that I am not drawn away. In Jesus' name, Amen.

Let's meditate on these scriptures:

1 John 4:1 ESV

Beloved, do not believe every spirit, but test the spirits to see whether they are from God, for many false prophets have gone out into the world.

Hebrews 4:12 DRB

For the word of God is living and effectual, and more piercing than any two edged sword; and reaching unto the division of the soul and the spirit, of the joints also and the marrow, and is a discerner of the thoughts and intents of the heart

1 Corinthians 12:10a NLT

He gives one person the power to perform miracles, and another the ability to prophesy. He gives someone else the ability to discern whether a message is from the Spirit of God or from another spirit.

As you reflect on today's topic, what do you believe God is saying to you?

A Prayer for Marriages

Lord, bless the marriages that you have put together. Let nothing and no one break them apart. Thank you for protecting them, safeguarding them and making them fireproof marriages that are able to withstand all of the highs and lows of marriage. Help husbands and wives to endure every season. Release your grace upon them to overcome every challenge. I bind the devil and all forms of witchcraft released upon the kingdom marriages in Jesus name. Help husbands to love their wives like Christ loves the church and help wives to submit to their husbands as unto the Lord. Let the love of Christ soften even the hardest of hearts. Heal every area of brokenness within the hearts of the husbands and wives. Increase their ability to understand, forgive, communicate effectively, be compassionate and love one another. Keep their love and passion for one another strong. Remove any and every person that his a hinderance to their marriage covenant. Let your order be established in their hearts, minds, homes and marriage. Place your love in the hearts of the husbands and wives and help them to respect one another and honor each other. Help them to overcome every obstacle that they may have to face.

And Father raise up healthy, lasting and loving kingdom marriages and families in Jesus name, thank God amen.

The Gift of Salvation

I want to take this moment to remind you that God loves you so much that he endured crucifixion to pay the price for your sins and defeat satan. He loves you so much that He allowed you to stumble upon this devotional and read this message telling you how much He loves you and has a perfect plan for you. Before you were born, Jesus left his heavenly estate to come down to earth and endure everything we deal with daily and more. And He endured and lived His life free from sin. Isn't that incredible? He didn't stop there...he was falsely accused by his people, spit upon, beat, and died the death of a criminal. But then something incredible happened: after He died and was buried in the tomb, He was resurrected from the dead three days later. Christ defeated death so we could live abundantly in Him while on earth. He died on that cross to pay the penalty for our sins....like, ALL OF THEM. If you believe this, ask Him to be the Lord of your life, forgive you of your sins, and begin following His teachings.

Pray this prayer with me:

Father, I thank you for revealing your Son Jesus to me. Thank You for sending Him to come to earth, endure the cross, remain sinless, defeat the enemy, and pay the price for my sins. Thank you for raising Him from the dead so I could live a resurrected life in Him. I want to live for you, and I want you to live in me. I believe in you, and I believe in your Son. I thank you for guiding me through the process to receive the gift of salvation. I believe that Jesus lived, died and was resurrected by God the Father. I confess this with my mouth and I believe it in my heart. I want to be saved from my sins and live a life submitted, yielded, and led by Jesus Christ. I thank you that by the faith you have given to me through your grace that I am saved.

Now, if you believed, confessed, and prayed this from your heart, you are saved :). Welcome to the Body of Christ.

Let's meditate on these scriptures.......

Romans 10:5-13

5 For Moses writes about the righteousness that is based on the law, that the person who does the commandments shall live by them. 6 But the righteousness based on faith says, "Do not say in your heart, 'Who will ascend into heaven?' " (that is, to bring Christ down) 7 "or 'Who will descend into the abyss?' " (that is, to bring Christ up from the dead). 8 But what does it say? "The word is near you, in your mouth and in your heart" (that is, the word of faith that we proclaim); 9 because, if you confess with your mouth that Jesus is Lord and believe in your heart that God raised him from the dead, you will be saved. 10 For with the heart one believes and is justified, and with the mouth one confesses and is saved. 11 For the Scripture says, "Everyone who believes in him will not be put to shame." 12 For there is no distinction between Jew and Greek; for the same Lord is Lord of all, bestowing his riches on all who call on

him. 13 For "everyone who calls on the name of the Lord will be saved."

About the author

SHANTA ATKINS is an inspirational power-house. Shanta is a vibrant and passionate woman who is gifted in singing, songwriting, teaching, ministering, and mentoring. She has a passion for lost souls. She has traveled across the globe singing, teaching, preaching, and building orphanages for children in developing nations for almost 20 years.

Shanta is sister to the "Grammy Award winning Gospel duo "Mary Mary" and is now blazing her own trail. After her success as a background singer and supporting vocalist she released her first single "I Will Follow" as a solo artist. With much anticipation she released her debut album "Follow Jesus" and continues to reach the masses with her voice.

As an influencer in media and podcaster Shanta has cultivated a growing online community through candid conversations and faith driven deep dives with her listeners. She engages her diverse audience with powerful words of wisdom and encouragement and her with her followers. Shanta continues to use her gifts, talents and experience in ministry to advance the kingdom of God.

www.ingramcontent.com/pod-product-compliance
Lightning Source LLC
Chambersburg PA
CBHW022112090426
42743CB00008B/816